2/23/2⁰

A-Z:

My Jesus Welcomed Encounter

When Divine Timing made Her Presence Known

Dana
I Love you
Thank you

WENEFER SERVON WHITE

Wenefer White

LifeRich
PUBLISHING®

LifeRich Publishing is a registered trademark of The Reader's Digest Association, Inc.

LifeRich Publishing books may be ordered through booksellers or by contacting:

LifeRich Publishing
1663 Liberty Drive
Bloomington, IN 47403
www.liferichpublishing.com
1 (888) 238-8637

Image Artist: Wenefer Servon White

ISBN: 978-1-4897-2657-5 (sc)
ISBN: 978-1-4897-2658-2 (e)

Print information available on the last page.

LifeRich Publishing rev. date: 12/17/2019

To my precious granddaughters,
Trinity and Claudia Servon,

"Write it on your heart that every day is the best day in the year. He is rich who owns the day, and no one owns the day who allows it to be invaded with fret and anxiety. Finish every day and be done with it. You have done what you could. Some blunders and absurdities, no doubt crept in. Forget them as soon as you can, tomorrow is a new day; begin it well and serenely, with too high a spirit to be cumbered with your old nonsense. This new day is too dear, with its hopes and invitations, to waste a moment on the yesterdays." ~Ralph Waldo Emerson

You both are amazingly beautiful, smart and wise!

PREFACE

I was very young, around four or five years old, walking down the steps of our front porch. I had my bottle, my trusted companion, in my hand. While preparing to indulge in another delicious and satisfying drink, my bottle was abruptly taken from me. Out of nowhere, the shadow of a person appeared. A familiar voice said, "You're too big for that bottle; you don't need it!" The next thing I knew, my trusted companion was tossed in the trash. I stood there, shocked. Suddenly, something vital to me was gone. I'm not sure what hurts the most, the loss of my trusted companion—my bottle—or that it was hijacked by someone I loved and felt safe with, my dad. I was thunderstruck. Imagine this being your earliest childhood memory.

You probably think *What a jerk,* he wasn't! On the contrary, I loved and adored my dad; he was my example of living a Christian lifestyle.

Somewhere in my brain, that unexpected reprimand by my dad triggered panic. At that very moment, my feelings were controlling my reality. My insides were screaming, "What are we going to do now?" This unwelcomed encounter became embedded in my early childhood psyche. Now in my sixties, this recalled the feeling of lost trust, possibly even feeling unloved, is still vivid. This childhood memory, along with other childhood experiences, shaped my future reactions (unconscious behaviors) and my responses (conscious behaviors).

The following is my backstory. I was brought up with deep-rooted Christian values. My father was an African American Southern Baptist minister who pastored for forty-six years. He and my mother were married for fifty-seven years, and from that union, they had six children, five daughters, and one son. I was the third daughter and named after my father. We were taught to believe that Jesus was the absolute solution to all life's challenges and the reason for all life's celebrations.

With that in mind, Let's begin.

I was at Walmart, waiting in line to pick up medicine. Standing behind me was a middle-aged woman. I turned around and said, "How are you doing today?" She replied, "Fine." We started talking and discovered we were neighbors, and that we both enjoyed walking. So, we set a time to meet the next day at the neighborhood park to walk the winding path of the walking trail.

We met at the park and started walking and talking. (It was a comfortable walk, slow and steady.)

She began to share some personal things about *me*. Something that only I would know. Things like the time I stayed with my mother's mother, Grandma Jessie. My sisters and Grandma at the time we're in the kitchen sitting around the table eating, but I was in the front room looking out the window crying, so hard, my nose started to bleed from becoming homesick, from missing my mother.

Then She reminded me of the time I was around thirteen years old standing in our back yard, with my hands on the fence, looking over the cliff, thinking to myself, if I yelled loud enough maybe my girlfriend that was playing at the bottom would hear me calling her name. Immediately I stopped walking and turned, looked her in the face, and said, "We have never met before. Who told you those things, and who are you?" With a luminescent glow, she gently touched my hand and replied, "Please don't be frightened. "All is well." Wenefer, don't be afraid, I bring you *Good News* because I am *HER*. I came here to ask you one question, "Who do you say that I am?" *She* asked me the same question, Jesus asked his disciples in Matthew 16:15, "Speaking to his disciples, Jesus asked, "But who do you say that I am?"

At that moment, unexpectedly, I experienced tranquility, such peace, that passeth understanding, a confidence I had never felt before; as a result, I proceeded to tell *HER*. ...

Jesus, you certainly are admired, respected, a decorated War Hero from many wars, and my closest Friend. My parents taught me to call on your name in the time of trouble, and their parents taught them the same. In churches, the name of Jesus is recited in prayers; and when friends and family gather to pray. Your name is called on for strength, guidance, help, deliverance, protection, forgiveness, and hope. I was raised to love you. And I do.

Your name will always be a subject of significant discussions, disagreements, and continual learning among theologians. I believe you tried to teach people about a principle that's higher than self. I believe you are more knowledgeable than an Oracle; You possess dominion and mastery; however, it seems your preference is compassion. You are the Promise from an invisible God that created all there ever will be. And, I truly believe you are the daughter of the Living God. **The End.**

Of course, this particular story never happened; I just wanted to make a point. To put it another way, each one of us has our interpretation of the scriptures. However, I truly believe Jesus was a man, a God-man, not a woman. But then, just a thought, would it had mattered to you if Jesus was a woman?

You probably won't be surprised when I tell you; my interpretation of God, Jesus, life, and spiritual things are broad. It's because of Jesus's teachings and Metaphysical philosophy; I'm living my best life. I will not raise hostility towards you over your interpretation of theology. (So, please offer me the same courtesy.) I believe there are two kinds of people. Those we get along with and those we don't. Most religions believe in a God of lovingkindness, grace, forgiveness, and mercy. However, all religions have extremists. For the greater good, I choose to respect and recognize glorification in all God's names. I share and celebrate goodness, grace, mercy, and love with you. Namaste

Nevertheless, Jesus did use unorthodox practices to reveal truths. Speaking for myself Metaphysical Christian teaching, brings a vision to my spiritual blindness, clarity to mental confusion, and liberation from fears and insecurities. Again, the above example was my way for you to see who I am spiritually so that the reach of the book is pretty easy to follow. By the way, thank you for your patience.

From this point forward, are real stories I've experienced, so seriously, let's get started.

Dad would often recite the poem "The A-Z Virtues of Jesus." After his death (transition), I began writing my interpretation of that poem. My A-Z stories of Jesus start with an alphabet followed by a word or two or a phrase that highlights the following story. At the end of each story, I ask you to reflect on a similar event and the impact it had on your life. I experienced these life events over my sixty-plus years. Some are funny while remembering others made me cry.

The following are the recitation of stories where something, someone, or the circumstance around me worked together for my good, a spiritual rendezvous. Henceforth, starting now when something or someone appeared at the precise moment, this occurrence will be referred to as "My Jesus Welcomed Encounter." Whereas, when the story is about perfect timing, this occurrence will be referred to as "Divine Timing made *Her* presence known." Regardless of the incident, I was delivered, made whole again, or received a blessing.

I purposely did not identify which spiritual rendezvous I encountered in each story. I welcome you to determine if it was "My Jesus Welcomed Encounter" or "Divine Timing made *Her* presence known."

It's okay if you don't agree with my Jesus upbringing or present-day truth. I'm not trying to convert you. I'm merely sharing precious memories, hopefully, to inspire you — however, my objective for writing this book is to challenge you to take the next step, to figure out whatever is in your mind and heart you desire to create or become. Make a decision. Then, create a flexible and workable plan that inspires you to keep your commitment to the plan. Nike's slogan says —"Just Do It." Likewise, Stephen Covey said, —"The main thing is to keep the main thing." My motivational thought is, "Slow and Steady is my process." Once I discovered my Muse, "something or someone that inspires," I was on my path of "Becoming," a published author. (My Muse: "Becoming," First Lady, Mrs. Michelle Obama, book)

Process, "a particular course of action intended to achieve a result." ~Princeton WordNet

Disclosure: These stories may not be the way they exactly happened, but they are the way I remember them to be. However, here's an indisputable fact.

We all must first learn our A-Z.

FOREWORD

Wenefer Servon White has created a collection of stories and memories that delight the readers heart and mind in such a way that you want to keep them close as reminder that life is so very precious.

She beautifully covers a wide array of emotions that causes the reader to stop, pause and think about this wonderful life we all share.

The reflections and questions posed in the "A-Z: My Jesus Welcomed Encounter" welcome you to contemplate the meaning of your own spiritual path while at the same time taking stock of life's simplest and sometimes most profound meanings.

The stories are authentic, the questions are provocative and the heart beneath each word is evident!

Reverend Richard Burdick
Spiritual Leader
Unity North Atlanta Church ~ Marietta, GA

ACKNOWLEDGMENTS

Without my Christian upbringing, there's no telling where I would have ended up; my parents taught by example. They lived their lives with a code of ethics and Christian values. They trained their children to have moral standards and to respect God, themselves, and others. Our parents also raised us to live a lifestyle of independence and practice the home-developed mechanics of self-care, that is, how to take care of ourselves and to be resilient.

I'm so grateful for my parents, Rev. Winfred C. Smith and Margarine "Margie" Knowles Smith, and for their many sacrifices and prayers. My siblings and I lived in a safe, loving, not perfect, but healthy environment. Our home centerpiece was learning about God, the Bible, Jesus, love, avoiding evil, forgiveness, faith, trust, memorizing Bible scriptures, and participating in church activities. Another essential value passed down to us from our parents was the importance of relationships, family, friends, and community.

At an early age, I learned my best friends would be my sisters—Gwen, Dorothy, Jessie, and Michelle—and my brother, Wayne. They're still my devoted friends. There's a tie that binds us; it's called unconditional love.

God blessed me with both a diamond and pearl, in my two beautiful, gifted children, Shively and Frank Jr. Two brilliant shining lighthouses came into my life and gave me another reason to get up in the morning, to work harder and smarter. We will always share our lineage and love. I will love you even when one day you look for me, and I will be gone. My beloved children, Resilience, *She* lives within you.

My anchor, best friend, and husband for over twenty years, we've become as two yarns loomed together to make a beautiful, one of a kind design. Even though we are independent thinkers, we have kept our commitment to—God, us, and family. Mr. Tony, you add value to my life. I love you.

To the reader, thank you for purchasing my book. As you read my stories, I pray you will be moved to laugh and cry with me; that you will be motivated to show someone goodwill by giving an unexpected blessing; and, I pray you may be inspired to share with others a precious memory.

And, to self, *Congratulations*! Writing this little book took five years. Despite the many distractions (*life*), I stayed focus by keeping the main thing, the main thing. I challenged myself to do whatever it took to write the next story by writing whatever was in my heart; I figured it out and typed. Be that as it may, it all started in my head with a *"voiceless whisper."* It asked a question, "Why don't you write your Jesus A-Z stories?"

May God, our heavenly Father, bless you even more than you could **possibly imagine.**

> **"You may delay, but time will not." ~Benjamin Franklin**

CONTENTS

When I was around eight or nine years old, Mama would keep chewing gum high up in a small pull-out drawer in the kitchen cabinet. I wondered, *why not treat myself to a slice or two of gum?* The possibility of any hurt or danger never crossed my mind, let alone of me falling. My strategy (process) was to stand on a kitchen chair placed next to the cabinet, open the glass door, and carefully pull out the small drawer.

1

I quickly pulled out the drawer, grabbed hold of the gum, and lost my balance. Spontaneously, the cabinet came tumbling down, as well as me! It scared me to death. There was such a loud noise; everything was shattered. Glass was everywhere. And, of course, I was left crying and screaming.

Everyone in the house came running to see what happened. Daddy was at work, so Mama and my siblings lifted the cabinet and found me with the package of sweet gum held tightly in my hand. I ended up with a couple of small scratches, no broken bones, and alive!

My family was so relieved I was not dead. While patching me up, Mama gave me a stern, "Don't ever do that again," talk. I received another stern rebuke when Daddy came home, followed by a big bear hug.

Reflection
Now, it's your turn. Do you remember a time growing up when you did something you shouldn't have, and instead of receiving punishment, you received a stern rebuke and a big bear hug?

B | BEDTIME

After our nightly bath, brushing our teeth, putting on our pajamas, Mama would braid our hair, and place a stocking cap on our head, so that our hair would look fresh and it would save her time in the morning.

We would hurry to the kitchen to sit around the table, waiting for her to give our treat. She would give each one of us, two chocolate sandwich cookies with vanilla cream in the middle (although we sometimes got vanilla wafers) and a glass of warm milk. My sisters and I would dunk our cookies in our milk, start giggling and teasing one another. Mama or Daddy would always say the same thing every night, and I do mean **EVERY NIGHT!**

"Eat your cookies, drink your milk, say your prayers, go to bed, no talking, and make sure you go straight to **SLEEP!**"

A sweet retreat this became for my sisters and me right before bed. Now that I'm much older, cookies before bed isn't a good idea because I'll get indigestion and rounder. However, saying my prayers before going to bed is a nightly ritual that will always be relevant and reverent.

Reflection
When you were younger, was there a nightly ritual, something you did before bed that will always be relevant and reverent? And, not make you rounder?

When I was about eleven years old, on a hot summer day, my parents called my younger sister, Michelle, and me outside. Right in front of us were two brand-new, shiny blue bikes. They said, "Here's something for you two." We didn't know what we had done to deserve such a big gift, a brand-new, shiny blue bike!

Looking back, I felt a sense of appreciation and joy. Remembering how hard our parents worked, I knew they sacrificed (paying bills, for food, and so on), but they still gave us an unexpected wonderful gift just

5

because they loved us. And, it wasn't even Christmas, Easter, or our Birthdays.

Remembering this act of kindness from my parents still puts a big smile on my face. Neither my parents nor Michelle are here any longer. However, in my mind, I see their faces, and in my heart, I can still feel their love. The powerful energy of love continues to transcend from one heart to another from the invisible world to a visible world. This transforming energy never dies. It continues to make a smile appear on my face and cause a fuzzy feeling in my heart even though it happened many years ago.

Reflection

Recall an act of caring. It doesn't have to be a material gift, such as a brand-new, shiny blue bike. It can be a simple act of unexpected kindness, something that made you feel a sense of appreciation. Does a smile appear on your face, and a fuzzy feeling fills your heart, even now? Could this possibly be how love feels? It's also called gratitude. We all know gratitude always replaces a lousy attitude. So, let's all remember to practice carrying a heart of gratitude. This way, we'll all keep the right attitude and walk around with a smile on our faces.

D | DETOUR

It was my turn to drive my three girlfriends to school, which was approximately forty-five minutes away. We were on our way home listening to music, laughing, and, of course, talking about boys. You know, girl stuff.

There wasn't a lot of traffic on the road. As the driver, I thought I had everything under control. However, our exit came up faster than I realized. The ramp was on the right, and I was driving in the far-left lane. Because it happened so fast, it's hard to explain what exactly happened. But this is what I recall. I quickly switched to the right lane, and all I could see was the yellow guardrail, which we were about to hit. And then suddenly, without incident, we made our exit. It was like I wasn't even doing the steering because I remember freezing-up and calling on Jesus.

Somehow, the car avoided hitting the guardrail. In a blink of an eye, I saw our lives coming to a quick end. But it never happened; instead, "My Jesus Welcomed Encounter" occurred and took over the steering wheel. Or maybe "My Jesus Welcomed Encounter" miraculously moved the guardrail.

We arrived home a little shaken, but safe and sound, inwardly knowing we had experienced "something." Possibly a miracle.

Reflection
Surely you can look back and reflect on a similar experience. It was like an out-of-body encounter. You saw your life coming to a quick end, but it never happened. How would you explain it? Possibly a miracle?

Mama packed a cooler full of bologna sandwiches, potatoes chips, cookies, soda, and water for our summer day trip to King's Island in Cincinnati, Ohio. Then Daddy loaded up the station wagon, and off we went. King's Island was an amusement and water park in the Kentucky-Ohio area.

It was known for its monster roller coaster. My sisters and I couldn't wait to ride it, although I felt a little uneasy. But, no worries! I was with my family, including my best friends, my sisters.

The man locked Michelle and me in the cart. And then, we started climbing higher and higher and higher; I started praying and praying and praying.

> Dear Jesus, help me! Please hear my prayer because I'm scared to death. Let me live through this scary ride and not die today. Help us to stay locked-in, and I promise I will never, ever never ride another roller coaster or anything close to looking like this scary thing for the rest of my life. In Jesus's name, Amen.

Of course, we survived. And to this day, I kept my promise to Jesus. I've never, ever never ridden another roller coaster or anything that resembles a roller coaster. Heck, I don't even take my granddaughters to amusement parks.

Reflection
If you have any monster roller-coaster stories? Feel free to share them with someone else.

Daddy pastored a small church about sixty miles from our home. Typically, one Sunday a month, Daddy invited another church to join us for the afternoon service. When this happened, Mrs. Sarah, a senior citizen church member, proudly invited us to her home for dinner. Man, oh, man, I couldn't wait for that Sunday feast. She had a long, rectangular table, covered with a beautiful white linen tablecloth. From her garden would be a vase full of freshly picked flowers sitting in the center of the table. Next to the white porcelain plate was a folded white linen napkin, shiny flatware, a tall glass filled with tea and ice cubes, with a lemon slice perched on one side. Dinner would include Turkey,

11

macaroni with lots of cheese, collard greens, corn on the cob, sweet potatoes, cornbread dressing, brown gravy, warm three-clover yeast rolls with butter melted on top, and for dessert, she would serve, butterscotch and lemon pie.

Even though the dinner was so delicious, she always served my favorite, a bowl of sweet potato juice, without the sweet potatoes. She would sit a bowl right next to my plate so that I could dunk those big warm yeast butter rolls into the sweet juice, which melted in my mouth, like a mouthful of warm candy.

Mrs. Sarah was my faithful friend.

Reflection
What sweet memory can you recall that melted in your mouth, like a mouthful of warm candy?

G | GOOD GOD

It was almost Easter, another Christian holiday to celebrate Jesus. In our family, it also meant new clothes to wear on Easter Sunday. We would go uptown to Belk's Department Store, where we purchased our new outfits. I clearly, remember this particular Easter dress so well! It was a light blue with a dark-blue cape attached. I loved it, and I knew everyone at church would too.

Easter Sunday finally came, and I was a Fashion Diva. You see, in our family, we had three sets of clothes:

school clothes, play clothes, and church clothes. I believe I was in the seventh grade, and there was going to be a Show-and-Tell Program at school in the coming week. Somehow, I convinced Mama to let me wear my new Easter outfit.

My teacher was one of my mother's many friends and our neighbor. On the day of Show-and-Tell, we were making signs using black ink. I was dancing around in my new Easter dress. The teacher said to me, "Sit down and stop being fast," which meant, stop seeking attention to yourself. As I walked back to my desk, my cape swiveled around and knocked over the bottle of black ink. The ink splattered on the floor, my desk, and my new dress! Oh, no! Please, God, let this be a dream, but it wasn't!

It seemed like it took hours to clean up all that black ink. Plus, the ink stains didn't come out of my Easter dress! The question was, how would I tell Mama what happened. I couldn't make up anything because my teacher was Mama's friend, and she would inform her that I was "being fast." Which that alone was enough to get me in big trouble with my parents. What on earth was I going to do? If only I were sitting down at my desk and paying attention to the teacher. But no, I was flipping around, showing off. What made matters worse, this happened right before lunch, so I walked around with black ink stains and wet spots on my new freshly stained Easter outfit during the lunch period.

Just imagine the teasing and jokes at my expense. I experienced two big emotions, humiliation and fear!

Upon arriving home, my mother met me at the front door and said in a sympathetic voice, "Let's get those stained clothes off you." I was shocked and wondered, *who was this strange woman? She's not my mother.* Still, I was eager to hear what Mama had to say. She told me the teacher called her at work earlier in the day and explained the class was making signs, and I accidentally spilled black ink on my dress, and the stains might not come out. She said it was just an unfortunate accident, and she would be willing to buy me another dress. Mama thanked her for the offer and said that it was not necessary.

That night ended with my siblings and me sitting around the kitchen table. What else, eating our cookies, drinking warm milk, saying our prayers, going to bed, not talking, and making sure we go straight to **SLEEP!**

That was the day I came to realize God is a good God! Thank You, Jesus!

Reflection
What God is a good God day, do you remember? And did you remember to thank him or her?

H HAPPY "SO GOOD, REAL GOOD" SONGS

Church attendance played a significant role in my childhood years. My parents made sure we were Saved. Which meant we accepted Jesus as our Lord and Savior. He would forgive us of all our sins (wrongdoings), and when we died, we all would be together again, living with Jesus in heaven.

Our Sunday consisted of Sunday school at nine o'clock, morning service at eleven, and back to church for afternoon service at three-thirty. We stayed for

BTU (Baptist Training Unit) at six and sometimes for evening service at seven.

Our church choirs would sing two songs that I just loved. They made me feel so good, real good.

To this day, I still get that same oh good feeling when I hear these songs. These two songs are "Holy, Holy, Holy," and "Higher Ground." They became my happy, feel-good songs.

The Senior choir would start singing "Higher Ground," it was a fast-moving energy kind of song, that got the church moving, folks on their feet, shouting, and praising the Lord.

And when all the Choirs—the Senior, Junior, and King Jewels Children—sang, "Holy, Holy, Holy! Lord God Almighty! Early in the morning, our song shall rise to Thee." I felt so inspired and so good, real good.

Reflection
Growing up, did you have a favorite song or two that inspired you and made you feel good, real good?

As I stated earlier, attending church and participating in the services were very important in our family. Not only did we go to church every Sunday (unless you were sick), we had to memorize scriptures, sing in the choir, and do anything else we were able to do in church for the Lord.

One Sunday, our pastor preached how the Lord, as a reward, would return more to those who gave to the

Lord. The scripture that morning was taken from the old testament.

> "Will a man rob God? Yet you are robbing me. But you say, how have we robbed you? In your tithes and contributions. You are cursed with a curse, for you are robbing me, the whole nation of you. Bring the full tithe into the storehouse, that there may be food in my house, and thereby put me to the test, says the Lord of hosts, if I will not open the windows of heaven for you and pour down a blessing until there is no more need." Malachi 3:8–10 ESV

After his sermon, he asked all the tithers to stand, follow the ushers to the front of the church, place their tithes in the offering plate, and then return to their seats; we followed his instructions.

Having said that, before the benediction, the pastor announced the finance officers would like to see me after church for a moment in the office. They said, "We have an envelope here with your name on it. We opened it up, but there was no money inside." I explained that after hearing the pastor's sermon on tithing and robbing God, I wanted to pay God. I thought I had put my tithe inside the envelope before I sealed it. So, I reached into my purse and handed over a dime, explaining that I was given a dollar earlier in the week. And how good it felt to know God was not going to curse me. Then I happily left the office, looking forward to my reward.

Reflection

Have you ever been scared into doing the right thing? And then happily, looking forward to your reward?

WITH GRATITUDE

Keep the Spirit in Your Heart ♥ Wington

THOUGHTFULLS™
© COMPENDIUM, INC. LIVE-INSPIRED.COM

J JUST LIKE THAT

In the summer, when our parents left for work, our older sister was left in charge of us. She became known as the 'Babysitter from he*ll*.'

Daddy always was the first to leave in the morning. And then Mama would wake us up. We would get dressed, make our beds, and eat breakfast. Then she would leave around nine-thirty and returned about four.

As soon as she left and was out of sight, the 'Babysitter from hell' put us out; to play in the hot summer sun. At lunchtime, she would call us back in to eat and use the bathroom; then the 'Babysitter from hell' once again, ran us outside to play in the hot summer sun. While *"The Wicked Witch of the West" laid on the couch (INSIDE) and watched Television. She had her routine down!!! So, we played for a while, and when we got tired, we stood on the porch, cuffing our little hands together, looking through the screen door watching what we could on TV. And like clockwork, she called us back inside and buttered us up right before Mama came home by telling us, "Y'all know, I was kidding. And you better not tell Mama." While writing this story, I realized something; the 'Babysitter from hell' was my first encounter with a bully, but then, maybe not.

Now, you may wonder why we didn't tell. We seriously thought about it and talked among ourselves, whether we should or not. Too afraid of what might happen to us, we didn't tell, nobody! So, day in and day out, we played outside in the hot summer sun, and when we got tired, we stood on the porch, cuffing our little hands together, looking through the screen door watching what we could on TV. However, after lunch one day instead of running us outside, something miraculously

---

* The Wicked Witch of the West, a character that played in the 1939 movie, The Wizard of Oz

happened! The 'Babysitter from he*ll*' said, **"Y'all don't
have to go** *outside*," then she turned the TV on.

Just like that, our older sister extended grace to us. And,
from that so-happy day, we sat on the floor, (INSIDE)
eating lunch together, falling out laughing, talking and
doing what best friends do, watch TV!

Rescued again by another spiritual rendezvous, "My
Jesus Welcomed Encounter," or should I say, "*Our*
Jesus Welcomed Encounter."

Reflection
Do you remember a time you experienced a sibling
rivalry that turned into a funny sibling story?

KING JEWELS

The King Jewels Children's choir director was so proud of us, and we were so happy to be called King Jewels.

There was a song we practiced repeatedly. The name of the song was "Ride on King Jesus." The Sunday morning came for us to sing, and I was about to sing the verse, but I got nervous, forgot the words, and froze. Just imagine standing there in front of the pastor and the whole eleven o'clock congregation, feeling embarrassed. Our choir director got so mad and upset she stopped playing, stood up, and said to all of us, "Sit down! All of you sit down!" The King Jewels embarrassed and looking silly, what else…sat down.

The pastor stood up and said, "Let us pray for our young people. We look forward to hearing them sing 'Ride on King Jesus' hopefully next Sunday." He gave us a big smile. In response, the church responded with a loud "Amen." After the service, we went on as if nothing had happened.

When all else fails, act as if nothing happened, kind of like *Dorothy, the Scarecrow, the Tinman, and the Lion singing "Ease on down the road." Only we didn't get to sing; we just sat down.

Reflection
When you experienced an embarrassing moment, and the spotlight was on you, did you freeze? Did you take it in stride and then eased on down the road?

---

* Dorothy, the Scarecrow, the Tinman, and the Lion, characters that played in the 1978 movie, The Oz

L | LOVE

Distinctly I remember this story as if it happened just a few days ago. I was around nine years old. While I was sitting on the side of our porch, playing pick-up sticks, Mama came outside and sat down beside me and said, "I'll play a game with you."

We giggled and had so much fun together. Such a precious sweet moment, just Mama and me playing a simple game of pick-up sticks on the side of the porch. I can still hear her say, "It's your turn now. Be careful." Mama is gone now; however, that moment still lives in my heart.

Emotion: *Love*

"We are born of love; Love is our mother." ~Rumi

Reflection
Do you remember an extraordinary time you shared with someone that made you feel loved, and oh, so special?

Down the street from our home was a funeral home. The funeral director and my mother were friends. I had been taking piano lessons for over a year and was beginning to play hymns. The funeral director asked Mama if I could come down to play soft music during a wake. A wake is when folks view the deceased, aka a Viewing. Typically a day before the actual funeral.

While people give solace to the grieving family, soft music is being played.

I suppose Mama thought this would be good training for me; she was probably looking ahead when I would play the piano for Daddy at church. So, she replied, "Yes, she would be happy to play."

On the contrary, I didn't want to play at any funeral home. (As a matter of fact, if I ever thought I would be playing at a funeral home, I would have taken up playing DRUMS, instead!) However, Mama didn't give me a choice. She said it was the right thing to do, and that dead people don't hurt anyone. And she did not want to hear another word about it. I was going to play, and that was that!

I remember it was a rainy afternoon. I started the slow walk down the street to the funeral home, carrying my umbrella, hymnal in my hand, and dressed in my Sunday clothes. As soon as I opened the door, I saw the piano positioned right behind the casket. Inside the coffin was a man in a black suit, lying there, motionless. I immediately ran out of the door faster than I came in, almost knocking over a basket of flowers on my way out. I ran back up the street, all the way home, crying and screaming, "I ain't going to do it! I'm not going to do it! Shoot, I ran out so fast; I dropped the umbrella, lost the hymnal, and by the time I got home, I was soaking wet!

I ran into the house and told Mama; I can't play for dead people! She called down to the funeral home and said she changed her mind about me playing, and she would need to find another piano player. That's when I discovered Jesus was a mind regulator. To this day, I do not doubt that it was Jesus who changed my Mama's mind. Or just maybe it was me running up the street deliriously screaming my head off, running into the house, and telling Mama, I can't play for dead people!

My mother and I never spoke about that horrible experience again.

Reflection

Do you remember a time when you met your fear head-on? Just wondering, how did you handle it?

Walking home from school with my girlfriends, we always kept a lookout for William, the class bully, and, unfortunately, another neighbor. He would jump from behind a tree and run after us, threatening to beat us up. We never said a word to any of our parents. After all, they wouldn't be there when William jumped from behind the bushes and beat us down. We all stayed on guard, watching out for William, the bully. Whenever anyone saw him, we all spontaneously started running all the way home without stopping.

Now looking back, it's strange, but William never caught us. Maybe he was pretending like he was trying to catch us because he just wanted to scare us to death and see us run, or perhaps we just outran him. Who knows, but William and the good Lord? All I know for sure, *"Divine Timing made Her Presence Known,"* because we saw Notorious William first before he saw us.

For sure, Jesus was with us because every time he jumped from behind those bushes, we ran so fast he never caught us. As I said earlier, maybe he didn't want to, but it sure felt like and looked like he did. Later, I learned typically, that's what bullies do, pretend like, look like, even act like they want a piece of you. A bully's main objective is to SCARE YOU! BOO! BOO! Are you Scared yet?

Reflection
Remember a time when you were under attack? Yet you made it through without a scratch, in spite of your fears? Kind of like the movie *Forrest Gump. Remember Jenny telling Forrest, "Run Forrest, run away, hurry!" Well, we were Forrest!

---

* Forrest Gump, 1994 movie

O ON-TIME

One of my friends was having a thirteenth birthday party at her house. There were more than twenty kids, dancing, laughing, and having a lot of fun. I had a boyfriend, and we planned to meet at the party.

We sat on the couch, holding hands and telling each other how much we liked one another. My boyfriend asked me if I loved him. When I told him I thought so, he said, "Prove it."

At that precise moment, my girlfriend called out, "Rev. Smith is parked in front of our house, blowing up his horn, waiting for you to come out." I immediately got up from the couch, ran outside, got into the car, and left the party. Daddy came at the perfect time. "Divine Timing made *Her* presence known." And I felt so relieved.

Although, I prove to my boyfriend how much I loved him. Enough to leave him sitting on the couch, wondering what just happened.

Reflection
Have you ever been in a very uncomfortable situation, not knowing what to do? Then suddenly, It happened, "Divine Timing made *Her* presence known?" And you felt relieved.

P | "PRAYER SERVICE" ON WEDNESDAY NIGHT

O n Wednesday night, we would go to prayer service at church and the laundromat. Mama attended when she could. Daddy would drop a couple of us off to wash, dry, and fold clothes. Before driving off, he would sternly remind us to "Mind your own business and leave everybody else's business alone," one of his many sayings. He would leave, taking the rest of the kids to prayer service.

My parents have transitioned to the next life now, so I think it's safe to come clean. I always preferred the local laundromat over prayer service. It was somewhat of a gathering place because it was right next door to the American Legion Dance Hall. Need I say more? Plus, at times, prayer service became too stressful for me.

On their knees, the deacons would start the first prayers, talking to God. Then each member took a turn to pray. The time came for Daddy to pray. Sometimes his prayers were so long and so intense. He would pray to God about how grateful he was to be a child of the King and ask God to continue to watch over and protect his wife and children, give him the strength to work, and so on. Daddy would become so emotional he would pass out flat! Yes, he would fall to the floor and be out cold. In our church, this state is called "Getting Happy," meaning the Holy Ghost overcame him. However, to me, it was quite scary to see him fall flat on his back, like a dead man, stiff as aboard. It kind of reminded me of the wakes at the funeral home, thank God, Daddy got up. Although getting happy lasted a few seconds or so, everyone would run over to fan him. He would wipe the tears from his eyes, telling everyone he was feeling fine, just fine. And everyone there knew he was telling the truth about "feeling fine, just fine," because most of them just finished, "feeling fine, just fine," too.

However, when it was time to leave with him, that was another story! After prayer service, I was scared to ride home with him, afraid he might pass out again while driving us home. I prayed that Daddy was through talking to God—at least until we left the prayer service, picked up everybody from the laundromat, stopped at Kroger's to pick up a few groceries, and returned home safely. Then he could talk to God. After all, Mama would be there so they could fan one another, and both of them could experience, like the title of songwriter, Lionel Richie, hit song of 1983, "All Night Long."... feeling fine, just fine.

Reflection
Ever remember being scared after someone talked to God?

Q | QUIET STORM

Whenever my sisters and I fought, Mama always did one thing, tell Daddy. And he would give us a spanking. He worked two or three jobs, which meant he sometimes came home late in the evening after we were already in bed.

It never failed. As soon as the house was quiet and we finally fell off to sleep, our bedcovers would fly off, and Daddy would give us a little spanking.

As I said, "It's always quiet before the storm!"

Reflection
What "Quiet before the storm" experience can you recall? Or maybe you don't want to remember. I certainly understand. Okay, let's pretend I didn't even ask that question.

R | ROCK

D addy's work schedule consisted of leaving early in the morning and sometimes coming home late at night. He worked on Saturdays too. But somehow, he found the energy to play with his kids, spend quality time with his family and study God's Word; and then drive more than sixty miles on Sunday to pastor a church with a handful of members.

Mama was our first parent to transition at the age of seventy-five. Daddy transitioned seven years later, at the age of eighty-seven, he retired from pastoring a few years earlier. He seemed superhuman, working long hours, caring for his family (including Grandma Jessie, who lived with us), attending weekly prayer service, taking us to the laundry mat, and finding the energy to pastor in another town.

To this day, I cannot remember him complaining about his hectic schedule. I recall, sometimes, he would come home looking tired and worn out. But as far as complaining, that wasn't his nature. In his children's presence, he never cursed nor took a drink of an alcoholic beverage. Nor can I say, I saw him mistreat anyone; he was an ethical, man of great faith, and jovial spirit. His commitment was to God, Mama, his children, grandchildren, and family. He also was a good neighbor.

Although he was somewhat strick, he was a lot of fun too. Have you ever heard the saying, "He's heavenly bound and no earthly good?" Well, he wasn't like that. Daddy was a fun person to be around. He loved to play checkers, tell jokes, laugh out loud, and always reminded others to "Always trust in God and forgive others," and, "Jesus is the very best, the very best!"

He was my example of living a Christian lifestyle. Daddy, my rock and hero.

Reflection

Name one upright person that comes to your mind who lived an ethical, moral, life of great faith with a jovial spirit.

S | STRENGTH

 One summer afternoon, my boyfriend and his two buddies stopped by my house. We were talking about the upcoming Labor Day party at another friend's beautiful home in the country. We were making plans to have a good time dancing, eating barbecue, and just having fun. They drove off fast, laughing, joking, and drinking.

When I awoke the next morning, Mama called for me and said she had some very sad news. She said, "There was a terrible car accident last night. The car hit a telephone pole, and everybody in the car died." Everybody was my boyfriend and his two buddies. It was the saddest day of my teenage years. At the time, it felt like an eternity.

All of them gone at one time, so suddenly and unexpectedly. What a tragedy! What a dark time for their families and our community. I felt sick, confused, angry, lost, and lonely. I was so young, about fifteen years old, and I remember wondering, *How on earth am I going to live?* I could hardly breathe without feeling emptiness.

Several times my parents sat down with me and talked about life's unexpected turns. They told me to trust in Jesus for strength because He will see me through. Daddy said, "You must remember a little bit of hope creates faith, faith creates trust, and trust creates knowing. The knowing is your belief that everything will work out. Eventually, in time, the pain will ease. It's okay to cry because you'll miss them. That's all part of the grieving and healing process. But don't' give up hope. There are no surprises to God; most of the bad stuff that happens in our lives is due to our own poor decisions and choices." While consoling me, they both hugged and wiped my tears.

They also spoke about the dangers of drinking and driving and poor choices that people make usually create adverse outcomes. Despite their counseling and support, I repeatedly had one thought: *If only they were not drinking, they would be here.* Whatever I thought, they made the unwise choice to drink and drive. Even knowing this did not ease my emotional and mental pain.

Years have passed, their funerals have come and gone. And now my parents and so many loved ones have gone on too. However, my parents' philosophy, "You must remember a little bit of hope creates faith, faith creates trust, and trust creates knowing. The knowing is your belief everything will work out" still holds for today.

Yes, the pain eventually went away, and all that's left are precious memories, and sometimes a wink from the other side, a beautiful reminder of your deceased loved one. My sister, Gwen, and I call these brief welcome encounters' a wink from the other side.

Reflection
Have you ever experienced something so sad and painful? You thought you could not get through

another day, especially another long sleepless night? What process did you use to recover and find peace?

And when was the last time you received a wink from the other side?

T | THANKSGIVING DAY

I vividly remember Mama's and Daddy's Thanksgiving Day house party. I'm getting out of bed with so much anticipated happiness knowing what this 'special day'

will bring. I must get the kids and myself ready to go to Mama's house for the Thanksgiving dinner. Finally, everybody is in the van and on our way. We're turning on 4th Street, seeing the familiar parked cars in front of the house, which brings the energy of excitement in our van.

There are my nieces and nephews, Christa, Dawn, Myra, and Charity coming outside to see if we need any help unloading the van. I see Sydni and Chase, playing in the yard. All the kids are hugging, laughing, they're just so glad to see one another again.

Sitting on the porch laughing and just catching up with one another, were my sisters, Gwen, Dorothy, Michelle; Jessie is holding her little girl, Ameka, and my brother Wayne holding his little son, Winfred.

Downstairs, Dad and my uncles are playing some serious checkers. Uncle Claxton and Uncle Russell are telling Daddy a joke or two, and he's falling out laughing. (Although, I believe they were trying to throw him off his next checker move.) Sitting around, talking, and laughing were my Aunts. They were continually asking Mama if she needed help with anything.

Mama's in the kitchen, taking hot buttered rolls out of the oven that I can't wait to eat!

Everyone has long anticipated arriving at this tradition of sitting down at Mama's beautifully decorated and mouthwatering table of delicious, beautiful food, and experiencing joyful family fellowship.

While holding one another's hands, Daddy, the Rev Winfred Smith, gives the annual Thanksgiving prayer:

> "Thank you, God, our Father, for my wife, our children, our grandchildren, our families, and friends. Lord, bless this food we're about to eat; may it nourish our bodies and uplift our spirits. Please keep us all safe from hurt, harm, and danger. May we show kindness to one another, forgive one another and always love one another as Jesus told us to do. Lord, we are so grateful to you for all our many blessings in Jesus' name, Amen."

Then, the Thanksgiving feast commenced!

Reflection
Can you remember a yearly family tradition that included the three F's: Faith, Family, and Food?

U | UNDERSTANDING

Although I grew up in a home learning about God, there was a season in my life; I became rebellious. It was my way of showing independence. I developed unhealthy relationships, ignored my well-being, and allowed others to manipulate my life, emotions, and self-worth. At times, I blamed others for my unhappiness, failures, and shortcomings.

Nevertheless, throughout my many ups and downs, right and wrong decisions, falling in and out of love, being criticized—whether it was deserving or not, in spite of all that, I continued throughout my life seeking God's love, guidance, and provision.

The Metaphysical study of the Bible has helped me gain more clarity of the scriptures. It teaches me to be open and nonjudgemental toward others. To me, Metaphysics teachings recognize and respect all of God's creation without the principles, rules, and dogma. It deals with the nature of one's overall well-being and mental healthiness. It has many areas of interest, such as philosophy, religion, meditation, etc.

> "People take different roads seeking fulfillment and happiness. Just because they're not on your road does not mean they are lost." ~Dalai Lama

The study of Metaphysics provides for me a bridge between religious dogma and spiritual freedom. It explores love, beliefs, spirituality, and humanness.

Whatever religion you associate yourself with, Metaphysics could contribute a broader knowledge of enlightenment. In my opinion, it provides a healthy self-focus on one's overall well-being; it's a lifestyle, not a religion; it emphasizes that most of the conditions in our lives are due to poor choices and indiscipline. I have become a less judgemental person because of the Metaphysical community and philosophy, which makes me a better Christian.

Healthy self-esteem, combined with humility, forgiveness, understanding, and unnecessary judgments, causes me to live ninety-nine percent of my days, pretty incredible.

Reflection
Picture each day as better than the day before. Imagine experiencing a wonderful (*not perfect*), but a wonderful day.

"Life does not have to be perfect to be wonderful."
~Annette Funicello

V | VICTORIOUS

B ecause of the Affordable Care Act (aka, Obamacare) in January 2014, American health insurance companies could no longer reject a person with pre-existing conditions. While being examined by my Optometrist, he discovered I had experienced a retinal detachment in one eye. In the other eye, the retinal was trying to detach as well. In the following months, I underwent several eye surgeries and the possibility of total blindness.

As a child, even into adulthood, at times when I became anxious, I would dream of being alone in the dark woods and being unable to find my way home. For several years, I shared this anxiousness reaction with no one. I later discovered I was experiencing panic attacks brought on by anxiety. Now, it appeared I would be facing my greatest fear, complete darkness.

I found strength and courage in God's word when fear came into my thoughts.

> "Now, faith is the assurance of things hoped for, the conviction of things not seen." Hebrews 11:1 ESV

Before my diagnosis, I had purchased a brand-new car, being unable to work; this unexpected medical expense only added to this emergency. My husband became our only source of income. As an automobile consultant, he works on commission. Also, during this time, America was experiencing several severe financial crises, as well as the automobile sector, which was facing financial hardship. He's worked in this industry for more than twenty-five years. But then something happened, "Divine Timing made *Her* presence known." The American automobile industry was saved and restored.

I wish I could thank President Obama, in person, and his administration who labored under so much hostility for the hard work and sacrifice put into creating the 2014 Affordable Care Act. Thank you all for fighting the righteous fight. You reconstructed a system that discriminated against Americans with preexisting conditions. And, thank you for rescuing the automobile industry.

Even though I have limited vision, the 2014 Affordable Care Act was there for my husband and me at the perfect time.

Reflection
"It is not *Happy* people who are *Thankful*. It is *Thankful* people that are *Happy*. ~Author Unknown

W | WAY MAKER

As stated earlier, I experienced several eye surgeries; there were times I could not travel because a "gas bubble" was surgically placed in my eye. Twice this bubble was placed in my eye, and each time, for at least two months (four months total), I was homebound with limited mobility.

During the time I could travel, my father transitioned. I was able to attend his funeral and be with my family, which was six hours away.

It has become apparent to me that whatever the reason for my challenges, it's all part of a higher spiritual evolution for my greater good and serves a necessary part of my spiritual growth.

That season of my life, I was going through significant changes. My daughter, son-in-law, and my grandbabies were relocating, although, now I can fly, then I couldn't. My father transitioned, and then the first of my siblings, Michelle, transitioned a few months later. This unsettling season of my life, all occurring within a few months apart, was very emotional. I became a robot, just numb. I tried my best not to complain to anyone because I felt everyone was doing the best they could. So, why complain? I remembered Daddy's words of wisdom, "You must remember a little bit of hope creates faith, faith creates trust, and trust creates knowing. The knowing is your belief everything will work out."

The following line comes from *Men in Black 3*, "A miracle is what seems impossible, but it happens anyway." *Good* in my life kept showing up!

---

* Men in Black, 2012 movie

Grace has a first name, **Amazing**, Amazing Grace, and said another way, Way Maker.

Reflection
In this story, which spiritual rendezvous would you say I encountered, either "My Jesus Welcomed Encounter" or "Divine Timing made Her presence known?" *It's open for discussion.*

X | X-RAY VISION

I was married to my kids' father for a long time. During the last years of our marriage, it became very rocky. Despite that, our family moved to another city. Nevertheless, we divorced.

Unknowingly, I was en route to meet my life-partner, Tony. From our first date, we became life-friends, now married for over twenty years. He's my present-day hero.

"...let there be spaces in your togetherness and let the winds of the heavens dance between you. Love one another but make not a bond of love: Let it rather be a moving sea between the shores of your souls. Fill each other's cup but drink not from one cup; Give one another of your bread but eat not from the same loaf. Sing and dance together and be joyous but let each one of you be alone. Even as the strings of a lute are alone though they quiver with the same music. Give your hearts, but not into each other's keeping. For only the hand of Life can contain your hearts. And stand together, yet not too near together: For the pillars of the temple stand apart, And the oak tree and the cypress grow not in each other's shadow." ~Khalil Gibran

Again, unknowingly, I would soon lose a piece of myself. And my peace-of-mind.

Reflection
Have you ever sacrificed for what you thought would become the greater good? And, the greater good turned out better than you imagine. God's blessings always outweigh life's challenges. Do the right thing and be blessed more than you imagine.

Frank S. Jackson, Jr.
Memorial Theological
Library

Approximately one year after our divorce, our son was diagnosed with cancer. He was fifteen years old. He went through several surgeries and months of chemo and radiation. The last resort was flying him down to MD Anderson Cancer Center in Houston, Texas, for evaluation. Recommended was an advanced cancer cocktail therapy. Then a few weeks after his advanced treatments, I heard the worst words I have ever heard in my life, "We're sorry, cancer has spread throughout his body, and there's nothing more we can do, there are no more options. Maybe he has a couple of months." I broke down and screamed.

After hearing such devastating words, No more options, and maybe two months left to live, the possibility of my child's death was horrifying! (This had to be a nightmare, but it wasn't) I was forced to make a decision. Either I was going to walk each day by faith or live each day in fear. Trusting in God was my response (conscious behavior). I discovered that faith is a spiritual, mental attitude — a mental discipline.

With the support of hospice, my amazing family, and dear close friends (Karen and Deborah) and others, Frank, Jr. came home. I lived off donations from churches and support from wherever I could find it. I was determined to continue to care for my children.

Inwardly, I trusted Jesus was carrying me through this very traumatic time. Throughout the coming days and the long sleepless nights, I prayed for peace, strength, and understanding for my daughter; for myself, I continued to ask for provision and guidance; for my son, I prayed for Divine healing. And I thank God throughout the day and sleepless nights for the help, support, and love we all received. One night while praying, I began to sense assurance; it came as a *"voiceless whisper"* in my mind, *"God will do whatever He chooses to do, with or without your permission or acceptance. Enjoy the present moments: I will provide for you. I Am the Giver and Taker of all life. Remember my words. And, trust me, all will work out."*

> "Trust in the LORD with all your heart,
> and do not lean on your own understanding.
> In all your ways, acknowledge him,
> and he will make straight your paths."
> ~Proverbs 13:5-6 ESV

Of course, I thought "work out" meant healed, despite the doctor's diagnosis. In spite of everything, it was an early Wednesday morning in February, when God called him, by his name, Frank, Jr., its time, to receive your heavenly reward. He left for what I wrote in his obituary, "A Call to the Highest Ground."

My deep, deep pain was unlike anything I've ever felt; however, it carried a subdued familiar sadness. Then it became apparent to me, my son's age at the time of his death was the same as my first boyfriend, killed in a car accident. This deeply embedded ache of years ago had reawakened. I screamed at God and asked, "How could I go through this again?" Only this time, it was more painful. This time, it was my son. This time, I would experience losing a piece of myself and my peace-of-mind.

Asking God for understanding, over time, I received clarity. I recalled how God carried me as a young girl through the emotional acceptance of the death of my young boyfriend and learning how to adjust to a new normal. I recounted the many times God's grace was my sufficiency; Yes, I had personal evidence that God would guide me through the darkness, once again. The ground I stand on must start with hope; then it moves to faith, moves to trust, moves to knowing, and arrives at the humbling footstool of gratitude. I could no longer deny, overlook, or take for granted, God. Looking back over the undisputed evidence of the footprints of the many times Jesus carried me, the many times God made a way out of no way for me, my faith was strengthened and renewed every morning, by God's tender mercies and lovingkindness.

I was able to stop work immediately and be home to care for my son, without the stress of holding down a job. God blessed me to birth him, mother him, and hear his last words before he drifted into a coma, lying in his room, decorated with his football, basketball pictures, and his many Nintendo games.

He said, "Mama, thanks for everything, thanks for being my Mama." and I told him, "Son, thanks for being such a wonderful son. I love you always." And I kissed his little bald head.

What I desired for my children was not riches, fame, or fortune but for them to be safe, healthy, wise, morally upright, to experience peace within, to feel valued, and to experience true love. God's grace gave me enough time to be strong enough to release him into the arms of the Creator of Love, God. Now, his new home is one of heavenly bliss in the protective care of love, God.

> "But, as it is written, "What no eye has seen, nor ear heard, nor the heart of man imagined, what God has prepared for those who love him."
> ~I Cor. 2:9 ESV

The following year after his transition, our beloved home church dedicated and renamed its library, The Frank S. Jackson, Jr. Memorial Theological Library. The library resides in the lower auditorium of the church. This small community church, Mount Nebo with a big open heart, offers an outreach ministry that continues to foster others, to shine their bright lights through spiritual education, mentoring, and to spiritually grow in a welcoming and loving community of Christian fellowship. What an awesome testimonial of a life that was short-lived, although he lived long enough for others to acknowledge his Christian character, appreciate his big smile, and his courageous life.

He was a brilliant shining lighthouse of strength, determination, and humility.

Even though he transitioned over twenty years ago, the gratitude I have for God has healed my brokenness. My resilience came from trusting in the Providence of God. What I heard when the *voiceless whisper* spoke to me, *"I will provide for you. I Am the Giver and Taker of all life. Remember my words. And, trust me, all will work out."* At the time I thought, I fully understood what God revealed to me. Nevertheless, God provided for my family. He kept his promise.

In loving memory of Frank, Jr.,

> "You were here for a moment...but left a lifetime of love." ~March of Dimes

Reflection
This story was the most difficult for me to write. I opened his cherry wood keepsake box filled with his special trinkets and treasures; his box hasn't been opened in years, feeling his presence, I experienced a soothing, spiritual elevation of overflowing Joy.

I'm sure you or either someone you know has lost a child. **I'm so sorry for your loss.**

> "Coping with the loss of a child is the hardest thing a parent can do. Without the help of the Lord, I don't know how we would have gotten through it."
> ~Mary Dillinger

Z | ZONE

It all started in my head with a *voiceless whisper...*

Voiceless Whisper: Remember how much your Dad loved to recite Jesus' attributes by using each letter of the alphabet? Why don't you write your Jesus A-Z stories?
Me: WHAT??? There I go again talking to myself.
Voiceless Whisper: Write your Jesus A-Z stories.

Me: Do WHAT? Anyway, I'm not a writer, even if I tried to write something, Oh forget it. Me, a writer? Anyway, how many letters are in the alphabet? Twenty-four or Twenty-six? Huh, this is crazy thinking! Let me get up from here and do something other than daydream.

Voiceless Whisper: Twenty-six .... There are twenty-six letters.

Me: Twenty-Six, What Twenty-Six things can I write about? Huh, Maybe **A** could be Amazing, **B** for Blessings, **C** Courage. Wait. Let me get this right; Dad already has an A-Z Jesus list, and why am I talking to myself? Let me get up from here and go to the gym or somewhere.

Voiceless Whisper: Write YOUR Jesus A-Z stories.

Me: What? Am I losing my mind, bored or something? Huh, let me think about this for a minute, Okay, I'll pray about it and include it in my meditation. Maybe I'll get some clarity, cause right now...Huh...It's just wishful crazy thinking; I just had eye surgery! I do well to see anything!

Voiceless Whisper: Stories, Twenty-Six, ABC Stories ... A Storyteller... A Storyteller. You can do it.

Me: A Storyteller??? I don't know twenty-six stories about anything! Maybe, I could write about growing up as a PK. I'm not sure I'm up to sitting at a computer all day. I'm sure that's not good for my eyes, typing all day on a laptop. Anyway, it sounded like a good idea. Just strange, though.

Voiceless Whisper: What's the rush? You're retired now, take your time, all the time you need, it doesn't have to be done in a week, month even a year. Write a little and rest a little. Write stories about growing up, your kids, Tony, family, Metaphysics, God, and it will be good therapy for you; YOU got lots of stories. You're a Storyteller. The only thing is, **I can't do it for you.**

The *voiceless whisper* was a God idea that I heard and followed through. I couldn't imagine after all these years, writing anything, especially a book. I wasn't planning on publishing it. I just kept typing, revising, typing, and revising. Then the *voiceless whisper* spoke again. "Get this published." I obeyed. And discovered a new Zone, *Storytelling.*

Reflection
What *voiceless whisper*, a God idea, you heard and did not follow through? A Chinese Proverb, "A journey of a thousand miles, must begin with the first step."

CONCLUSION

I've discovered by not blaming others for my unhappiness and unfulfillment allows me the space to develop an accountable friendship with myself and God. And to become an advocate for my overall mental well-being, as well as my peace of mind. When teachable moments occur, I try not to lose my temper and self-confidence.

"If you have a lemon, make a lemonade."
~Dave Carnegie

Whether a lack of discipline, fear of judgement from family and friends, or procrastination whatever has held you back from experiencing your best life, the needed changes requires you to embrace your truth, and then accept it without excuses. You know, I didn't know what I liked until I first admitted what I didn't like in myself. Then, and only then was I able to make the necessary changes. I found peace of mind; I experienced a joyful spirit and improved quality of life.

I'm in my sixty-fifth chapter of life and still spiritually growing, learning how to discern the *"voiceless whisper."* When I'm unable to harmonize with others, I change the channel (meaning move on) without the guilt. After reading my anecdotes, you've discovered, I'm just like you. I've had good days and long sleepless nights. In spite of everything, life is about "how-to" effectually handle and learn from the many encounters one experiences in life.

However, I caution you, embracing your truth, may bring about a significant shift in your life. You may discover its time to change where you attend church or assembly or take a break from attending. Maybe you'll become truthful about an unhealthy relationship, and begin to value who you are, then happily turn the other cheek to see what's going on in that direction, you may have been overlooking a really caring person. Or simply enjoy time with yourself. Who knows? You may awake the sleeper in yourself. Did you know that new thoughts create new ideas, which lead to new opportunities, new courage, a new you, a new dance!

> "God, grant me the serenity to accept the things I cannot change, to change the things I can, and wisdom to know the difference." ~Reinhold Niebuhr

To me, the essential part of this poem is, "God, grant me the serenity." In other words, God grant me stillness;

God grant me time to prayer, to meditate and courage to do what it is or is not for me to do. I'm asking God for a spiritual awakening, an intervention, a direction, and strength of mind to do what is right for me.

Yes, both Metaphysics concepts and Christian teachings/beliefs bring me the peace to evolve. They keep me on my path of divine order, inner harmony, and nonjudgment. I'm here to experience as much joy, peace, and fun as I can. At times, it may require walking away from what or who I cannot change, the courage to change what I can (myself), and resilience to keep moving forward expecting *better than* I could ever imagine outcomes in every area of my life.

My spiritual rendezvous, "My Jesus Welcomed Encounter," or "Divine Timing made *Her* presence known" are where the intersections of my humanness and spirituality came face-to-face, manifesting from the invisible to the visible results for my good.

> "...I've learned that whenever I decide something with an open heart, I usually make the right decision. I've learned that even when I have pains, I don't have to be one.
>
> I've learned that every day you should reach out and touch someone. People love a warm hug, or just a friendly pat on the back. I've learned that I still have a lot to learn.

I've learned that people will forget what you said, people will forget what you did, but people will never forget how you made them feel." ~Maya Angelou

Namaste

"The definition of Namaste (pronounced na, ma, stay) is both a physical gesture and a spoken spiritual salutation, which is the recognition of the divine spirit (or soul) in another by the divine spirit in you."

- *Living Words of Wisdom for a Happier, Healthier You*

DADDY'S A-Z POEM

Rev. Winfred C. Smith

July 21, 1926 – June 25, 2014

1. He is ABLE to keep me.
2. He is BLESSING me every day.
3. I know God CARES for me.
4. He is my DIRECTION.
5. He is an EVERLASTING God.
6. He is a true and FAITHFUL friend.
7. He is a GOOD God.
8. He is HIGH and HOLY.
9. He is INSPIRATION.
10. He is a JUST God.
11. He is the KING of my life, and He has never left me alone.
12. He is a LOVING God.
13. He is a MIND regulator.
14. I NEED him every day and every hour.
15. He is always ON Time.
16. He is a PRAYING God.
17. He comes in the QUIETEST hour.
18. He is my ROCK of ages.
19. He is the STRENGTH of my life for today and tomorrow.
20. He is a God that you can TRUST.
21. He is a God that UNDERSTANDS me when I'm right, and when I'm wrong.
22. He is a VERY present help in times of trouble.

23. Yes, my brothers and sisters, I know that he is a WAY MAKER.
24. He has an X-RAY vision. God sees all and knows all.
25. He is YOUR joy for today and tomorrow.
26. Yes, God has a ZONE, and when I seem to get out of line, God let me know that He is my Father, and I am his child.